MW01275402

Poets Table
Anthology

SCW
Publications
Seattle, Washington

Copyright ©2002 by SCW Publications
Manufactured in the United States of America

Library of Congress No. 2001 132929
ISBN 1-877882-27-5

First Edition
Copyright reverts to authors upon publication. All rights in this book are
reserved. No part of the book may be used or reproduced in any manner what-
soever without written permission except in the case of brief quotations
embodies in critical articles and reviews.

Cover art: *Table for Poems* (1958) by Richard Gilkey
Special thanks to Basyl and Ann D. Kercheval of Seattle for permission to photo-
graph this wonderful painting and use it as a cover image for this anthology.
Basyl Kercheval met the artist in the 1950s at the Blue Moon Tavern in Seattle
where Gilkey, Theodore Roethke, and other freethinking artists, writers and
poets often gathered. The painting, done in oil on canvas, may have been
inspired by the artist's association with the poets. In 1970 Gilkey (1925-1997)
moved from Seattle to the Skagit Valley, the inspiration and source of his well-
known landscapes.

Cover Design by Mike Jaynes

SCW Publications
1011 Boren Ave. #155
Seattle WA 98104
206.682.1268
info@poetswest.com
www.poetswest.com

Contents

Introduction

Poets Table began in 1997 as a loose association of ten poets who had completed the advanced poetry course offered by the University of Washington Extension Classes. For several months the yet unnamed group met in members' homes, critiqued each other's work and did poetry-writing exercises.

In 1998 the group moved to Wit's End Book Store and Tea Shop in the Fremont area of Seattle. Amid the children's books, the biographies, and the collections of poetry, a sort of poets' table developed. Of the ten original poets, Pat Duggan, J. Glenn Evans, Murray Gordon, Carol Shaw, Leonard Tews, and Rodney Williams remain as active members. They were joined by five new members: Nancy Dahlberg, Michael Magee, Laura Snyder, Jennifer Rickards, and Pieter Zilinsky.

Several Poets Table members are active in the Washington Poets Association and serve on its board of directors; they also are active in *Poets*West, serving as advisory board members and as judges for the *Poets*West Reading Series at the Frye Art Museum. The Poets Table members have read their poetry at many venues, including the *Poets*West events, Words' Worth readings before meetings of the Culture and Parks Committee of Seattle City Council, and other local venues.

Some of the poems in this anthology began as writing exercises or timed-writes critiqued by the group. This collection represents a diversity of voices, visions and styles. In this way we keep the Poets Table open to change. The circle has widened to include you, the reader.

Michael Magee and *J.Glenn Evans*

Nancy Dahlberg

Where Are We Now?

Arturo's eyes met mine in the mirror, shone dark
in his full-moon face and he smiled, slow-touching
my head the way a mother might feel her child
for fever, his fingers combing through my hair,
yellow silk, the slow lift and fall. Massaging
my scalp, his hands coaxed cinnamon suds,
slipped on orange-blossom rinse, then swaddled
my wet head as though it were a cherished infant
and led me back to his station with its mysterious bottles,
gleaming scissors, tortoise-shell combs—promises
of transformation—where we exchanged the confessions
that pass for conversation. Ah, a fellow Texan, he said,
a soft Chicano accent emerging as he spoke
of childhood in El Paso and his barrio near the river.
I told him once our car broke down there,
my discomfort with the Mexican mechanics
who laughed and spoke words I couldn't understand.
When he parted my hair, one side against the other,
I was afraid of the scissors in his dark hands
slashing away blond curls that fell to the floor,
smothering the straight dark hair already there.
I felt he could see through me in the mirror,
knew I believed he meant to cut each hair
a different length, all of them going nowhere
so that I looked like I had swum a river,
been waked out of sleep by blinding light.

I Was Tired of My Own Voice

I wonder where I'm going always searching
for that final line of closure to make sense
out of everything that's gone before

like hard candy made from boiled sugar, water
flavored orange or peppermint, cools and hardens
to final object out of process.

No wonder disappointment with odorless
roses or salt-free pickles, expectations
not met. Life lived in the mind, a waste

of flesh, its sensory pleasures. Let me take
your hand, your fingers warm and locked in my own,
lead you, silent, up a mountain trail,

to leave small earth-scars, our breath giving moisture,
visibility to the air—temporal
evidence of our existence there.

We will not speak. Words meaningless in that place—
only skin, muscle, bone to recall the heart,
its damage or its promise to heal.

Confirmation

Her own door locked, key neon-spiralled on her wrist,
Mother roams the rooms at the nursing home,
accuses fellow residents of stealing her incontinence pads,
Madeira cookies, scatter pins, anything she can't remember
having used or eaten or squirreled away. Yesterday,
to grey heads bobbing over cream-of-wheat and runny eggs,
she complained that her children wrote large checks on her account,
have stolen her money, then hinted no one there is safe,
poison could be in the food. Mary choked
and dropped her orange juice, arthritic Leota
refused to swallow the Nuprin, and the manager called
with, *please, we need another talk.* Lies,
my mother says, all lies, then weeps and mutters
her curse, the rest of us should live to be so old.
Every day she gives the office two weeks' notice
she's moving back to the old neighborhood,
where what she needs she can walk to, even though here
a walk to the door is exhausting and once outside,
she's lost. Mother can't remember how she forgot to eat
and ended up at Lutheran General, a mirrored counter
where her sofa should have been, the trees outside
replaced by a five story building; and after
she went home, the familiar rooms strange,
nothing remembered, not even old photographs
I unboxed, thinking she at least had her past.
That day I handed her the portrait of herself at twelve,
head tilted toward white-flounced shoulder,
one hand on her hip, full lips closed in a smile.
Is this Maggie? she asked, meaning my youngest daughter,
and turning the picture over, read the strong slanted hand
on the back—Irene, 1914, Confirmation. *My mother
wrote that*, she said, and pleased this time, looked
again at the young girl, her pale eyes bright.

The Leap

A span over water, a jumping-off place
with or without wings. Imagine her leap
into air, face and chest lifted toward blue,

arms outspread, the rush of a whole life
left behind on a bridge somewhere between
here and there. Haven't we all wanted

to jump out of our bodies,
the trappings of gravity,
free skin and bones and hank of hair,

experience the free fall and cleansing air
before the bright white light
to come back to this world as a meteor flash,

a noble fir splitting the wind, or an owl
calling a beloved's name—spirit returned
to say *I am here, I am still with you.*

In Our Time

Simmering pink morning slips away
disappears into water, becomes water,
cool and gray like your eyes. I imagine
their cold gaze now that summer's gone,
what's left of fall frosted over
brown leaves matted underfoot, drooping
chrysanthemums beaten down
rain driving mildewed petals into mud.
No longer close, we send messages
by mail, letters damp with fog, a cold delivery.
We were like children once, took pleasure
bobbing in the bay's waves,
water warm under Galveston sun
and our own heat. If I believed
in second chances, I would play
the game again but not get caught
in desire's undertow. Now,
I prepare for winter, look for warmth,
kindle a fire inside.

Would It Be Possible?

I've heard it's possible to learn the truth
lying alone on the shore, facing
failed love's chill of memories and sighs.

All my love's been raw and hard to swallow,
mostly underwater, rarely coming up for air.
Truth smells of dill-weed and distant rain;
the soul's tonic invasive,
altering the blood, thick then thin,
torment's internal balancing act.

        Transforming,
the way your logic invaded my mind
like tap shoes' clack on marble floors
echoing through mirrored corridors.

        Honesty
felt like a labyrinth inducing panic
or a heart-rush, palms refusing surrender.

        What does it mean
to walk away from the struggle, to deny
the wisps of wisteria alive with bees?

The pond's moon-swarms reflect love's ambivalence—
was it seaweed green or reflected mauve
that blurred my vision?

Would it be possible to start again,
wash away the sand and come back clear,
see through myself to you?

Righting the World

Upside down, my first world view,
no wonder I keep trying to get it right,
imagine walking on the ceiling—
ladder-back chairs rooted above,
something to chin on
or climb toward heaven's floor
while the globe spins stories
of what little I've seen. Yesterday,
the sun appeared, first time
in weeks, along with two lawn chairs
outside the apartment behind mine.
Two women dressed in black relaxed
in the warmth and I wondered what stories
they told or if they spoke at all.
Sometimes in this misted region
the sun itself passes for conversation
or a day's writing. From morning to afternoon
sunlight and shadow erase each other
until the page is blank and the stories,
like breath withheld, catch in the throat,
then spill out in a sigh of relief
or regret. Today, a Sunday,
I woke to the scent of distant rain,
went out to early mist,
praised the gods of irony and wet air.
All shadows had disappeared and I laughed
as if nothing had ever gone wrong.

Pat Duggan

My Daughter is Becoming the Moon

My daughter is becoming
The moon.
I see it seeping in
Her sapphire skin,
Her face
Alive in its glow.

My daughter is becoming
The grass.
I watch it lapping at
Ten opal toes
As her legs
Begin to grow.

My daughter is becoming
The wind, the rain.
I see them hoisting her
Up then holding her back
To scatter diamonds
Through her hair.

My daughter is becoming
Herself.
I cringe as she pushes
Past brambles and thorns;
Her hand becomes a rose.

Maternal Instinct

Fragile, wet bird of mine without feathers,
I hold you, stroke the china cup of your chin
And watch these moth wings of your heart beating

So wildly against the marbled blue cage of your chest.
I inhale this dense warmth of you rising off skin
Like the steamy breath of rain-soaked gardenias.

As our two heads weave now in strangely separate orbits,
I reach out to claim you as moon only to realize
That my first act as your mother was to push you away

As hard as I should.

Summons

You prowl
Through my heart
Mac tíre.*
You track my every move;
Day brings only a restless shadow;
At dusk I sense you poised,
Ready to spring
Over the fences of sleep,
Feed in the crevices of dreams,
Lead me to this hilltop
To show why we've come here.

And just when I think I know
The answer,
Just when you open your jaws
Wide enough
To swallow the moon,
I hear instead
My own heart
Howling.

*wolf (Irish) "mac cheera"

Borders

First time ever crossing an official state border
By car from Washington to Oregon,
My nine-year-old mind expected a thick red line.
I wasn't entirely disappointed,
Only guessing wrong about the color.
The Columbia River painted its line blue
And wide enough to leave no doubt
Where one place left off and the other resumed,
Ensuring that this distance always remained
The same, holding these lands together
While pushing them apart. After that,
Borders always disappointed
Though I still kept looking for lines.

When I return to Ireland,
Border checks between the North and South
Are gone, plowed under these fields,
Their imposing stalks
Replaced by ground hugging crops,
Not dependent on furrows to thrive,
Tractor sewn seams no longer in evidence.
Though each town still appears
To have its official guard
Watching from the cottage window,
Supervising the comings and goings,
Only the wind now seems to whisper
The obligatory question, "Why are you here?"
And where is here? I can't answer, lost now
Without these familiar checkpoints.
My borders, too, have disappeared.

Final Boarding Call

"We're in the departure lounge now,"
She often joked, referring to their ages;
Stamped pension books, their one-way tickets.

A month later, she would board the plane
By way of ambulance and hospital,
Still travelling on standby.

"I hope you're not planning to leave me,'
The husband said in alarm.
"I'm doing my best to stay," she replied.

But that night a seat came available
And she couldn't resist taking it.
Her suitcase had been packed for years.

The husband sits alone now
In the departure lounge
Waiting for the next flight out.

Stone Harvest

Even then, there was a silence shared between us
Stretched like the bed sheets we slept in,
Pulled taut as ice across a pond.

In December's veins of moonlight I watched
Your face, the one that spoke more to me
From underneath its mask of sleep.

Your eyes—the way they used to look at me,
A gentleness I could only know now
When both your eyes were closed.

Daylight would bring still longer shadows
In a winter that we began a spring ago
Which should have been a time for planting.

And was. For even in this barren chill
Of marbled silences,
My other lips would speak a child.

Pesky Twin Sisters

These two mosquito bites
Festered,
Tormented,
Took on a life
Of their own.

Ignored their minder
Who took them everywhere,
Caused embarrassment
By popping off her shirt buttons,
Just to be annoying,
Stuck out their tongues at boys,
Then hid and giggled,
Refused to be constrained.

When they were older,
Made fools of themselves
Again. Pregnancy did it;
They were full
Of themselves.

In old age, they're no better,
Looking down their noses
At everybody else.

J. Glenn Evans

Eighteen-Ninety

When the spring blossoms fall like winter snow
Thoughts come of the snow at Wounded Knee
There is a picture of Chief Big Foot
Who lies frozen like a statue in snow
Body raised up, bundled against the cold
Looks alive, but lies there dead
In this white man's picture of a death pose
Looks like he might get up, but he's gone
Dead and frozen and all alone but for
A horse and two white men who look on
Gone are the Gatling guns and the soldiers
The two hundred fourteen dead Indians
That included one hundred and seventy-seven
Women children, which tidied up this scene

Lost Shadows

A favored river walk in the deep woods;
Temples of God I often called these trees.
To build such a place - only God could.
Refuge for God's creatures that are still free.
In the spring - in the summer - streams of light
Pierce through windows of the tall tree branches.
Rays of gold and silver from heaven's height,
God's fingers that point to man's last chances.
Then one summer I took this hallowed walk;
Parched grass dead moss and only insects played.
Overhead flew a circling hawk
Where once a sacred ancient forest lay

The giants of old were not to be found,
Only their shoes were left upon the ground.

Bill and Sherry

As a timber cruiser
once I trod
a private Northwest wood
in the year of 1925

I chanced upon a tree
a douglas fir
that stood tall
among its friends
but no taller than they
Under its bough
picnicking alone
was a young woman
not more than 25
Not to disturb her
I quietly passed by

Later I came back
to cruise that spot
and on the trunk of this fir
were carved two names
Bill and Sherry
1917

This forest glen
was scheduled for clear-cut
I flagged that tree for no-cut
She might have been a young lass
that had been there with her soldier

Many years past
and on that same day
in April
I took my grandson
to view a new forest
in that area
where I had been
so long ago
There tallest of them all
stood that douglas fir
that I had spared
and still for all to see
were the faint markings

Bill and Sherry
1917
Sixty-three winters had passed
It was now 1980
Under the bough
where once had picnicked
that young lady
rested a grave
where was carved
on a marble marker
an epitaph

Sherry Cochran
1900 - 1975
Buried with the spirit
of her Bill
who rests in a French field
with his comrades

Morford Mann

Snow began to fall
The north wind
Made it cold
I just stepped off
The Greyhound Bus
In the mining town
Of Wallace Idaho

A half a block
To the north
I saw the depot
Of Burlington Northern
All closed and dark
I walked the opposite way
The lights of Sweet's Cafe

Came into view
Through the falling flakes
Slightly sheltered
Standing in front
Was a strange man
Who looked like Morford Mann
He stood there in the cold

Old shriveled and gray
Three days growth of beard
Stained by juice
Of tobacco leaves
Thirty years
Since last I met
This Morford Mann

What was
Morford Mann
Doing way out West
We both grew up in the East
Mortal enemies then

He terrorized my childhood
Bloodied my nose on school grounds

Chased me home from school
And bullied me so
This Morford Mann
He stood
In direct line
Of my approach
I stopped in front of Sweets Cafe

And looked him in the eye
I said nothing
Just looked at him
With a glare
He looked back
And I expected a poke
Or to even be

Put to the touch
I could see his mind
Transcend the years
His eyes brightened
Like he had seen
A long lost friend
Tears came into his eyes

His voice choked
Then I heard him say
Jack
He gave me
A bear like hug
His body throbbed
As I heard his cries

Artful City

> A world God never made
> —George Nelson, *How to See*

Silhouette man pounds air with hammer
While Blue Moon's man drinks his can of beer
And dinosaurs at the waterfront
Take nips at the world's newly-mades

Downtown a building once stood on its toes
Until stone salal covered its shoes
Down the street men run for love of lore
And Sir Henry's backbones stand their ground

Mammoth snails move under the city
And pause at Marilyn Monroe's station
While Detroit bugs crawl in line above
Shiny discards for another time

Noguchi's donut at Volunteer Park
That even hungry artists will not bite
Purple gold silver red and some blue
Undulate from Queen Anne's soft rock

In Laigo's universe at Seattle U
Genesis meets big bang's evolution
Raven sits atop Tlingit totem
With moon in its beak to light the night

Corporate tags a sign of the times
Like graffiti that oozes from the night
Space needle holds its head in the sky
Poetry echoes from cellars to Frye

The Apple Tree

Old woman gnarled and twisted
Like the apple tree out back
Four score and three her eyes
Had scanned that scene

Useless and worn, she wished death would come
She would open the door and welcome him
Sipping her tea, she remembered
A can of arsenic in the tool shed
Her man once dusted potatoes leaves
Gone were the potatoes and so was he

A smile crossed her cheek
Green crystal vase that sat upon the highboy
Once held boughs of that apple tree's
First spring blossoms
She had once climbed that tree and torn her dress

She got up and went to the tool shed
She came out with an old garden saw
Slowly she cut two small boughs
Carried them in and filled the green vase
With wet spring blossoms and placed them at her side

My Father's Hands

Were large and equal to the task
Held the plow handles, chopped corn with the hoe
Fed his family and the stock all year long
Planted peanuts and picked the cotton
That bought the school books and the clothes
They chopped the wood that warmed us all winter
Never spanked, but those large hands kept the rules

When war came they made artillery boom
Bludgeons in Battery A boxing ring
North Africa, they set Hitler straight
South Pacific, sent the Japanese home
His brother's hands stayed home, made a fortune

After the war my father's hands were set
To the task of pitching uintaite
Worked on the Colorado high plains
Rarely were they ever folded in prayer
But like God's they were there when needed
Now they lay at his side, wait the next task

Murray Gordon

Get to Know Your Jacket

Reach into the closet for your jacket
and grasp the collar which was sewn on by
Nan. She has a quota of twenty-eight
dozen per day. Thrust a hand into one
sleeve and twist the other hand into the
second one. They were set by Sideth and
immediately after topstitched by
Chong. Their machines are adjacent but they
are not allowed to speak to each other
for forty hours a week, fifty-two
weeks a year. Smooth the jacket around your
torso. Larita bodyseamed it for
you. She's been doing that job for more than
fifteen years breathing in lint all that time.

That the left and right fronts of your jacket
should match, Khamdy personally took a
marking pencil and marked your zipper at
the neck, yoke and waistband. Last year, she set
61,405
front zippers. The pocket welts were cut by
Eulalia who stands on her feet for
eight hours a day at the Reece machine.
The pocket zippers were set by Honee
who is so good that you will never
see a pucker at the corners because
she must make repairs on her own time. When
you put your keys, comb and change into
the pockets, you can do so with confidence.
They won't fall through because Jojo is the
pocket bagger. She is so fast that it
isn't necessary for her to think

anymore. William cut out the pattern -
360 ply. There is
not a moment anymore when he does
not hear the buzz of the cutting machines.

Pauline supervised the sewing line. They
gave her a raise, put her on salary
and now they don't have to pay her over-
time when the plant works on Saturdays. George
is the owner. He comes in late and leaves
early, takes two hour lunches and he
does not know the names of any workers.

Your jacket comes as an experienced
traveler. Ordered in Seattle from
a catalogue company in Maine, the
fabric was shipped from a Massachusetts
mill to the contractor in Seattle,
reshipped to a subcontractor in North
Carolina, sewn there and reshipped back
to Seattle to be inspected, tagged
and bagged, reshipped to Maine and then shipped to
your home address in Seattle. When you
wear the jacket no one will be able
to see any of this. What they will see
on the left front is a small label with
the name of a dead man woven on it.

The Numbers Game

In the first place
He was a second story man.
With his third eye
He worked for the fourth estate
To expose the fifth column
With his sixth sense.
He was the seventh son
And played only the eighth notes
Of the ninth symphony
On tenth avenue
At the eleventh hour
Of the twelfth night.

She was first class
Second to none
And rode the third rail
Into the fourth dimension.
She was no fifth wheel.
Playing the sixth scale
In the seventh heaven
She was the eighth wonder.
In the ninth inning
She recited the tenth commandment
At the eleventh hour
On the twelfth of never.

They met at the first light of day.
And with no second thoughts
Danced the last dance.

Listen

As you listen to Albert, he opens his wallet to show you a yellowed news-paper photograph. Paris. Summer of 1941. He is in uniform, handsome, not yet twenty and the world is his.

Albert goes on. The town is in ruins. I crouch at the end of the bridge. Bullets crack and whine all around me. Men shoot. Run. Fall. Kneeling from cover, I fire my machine pistol. Ch ch ch ch chatter chatter. My bones chatter in the late September heat. Crack. Whine. Crack. Whine. Then nothing. Then something stings my leg. An insect? Debris? You never hear the bullet that hits you. Everything becomes as still as a photograph. The world stops. I try to stand up. My head won't move to look down. Maybe if I don't look this world won't be there. But blood pours over my gray trousers. I am hit. I am shot. I've taken a bullet in the leg. First I am numb. Then I feel someone clutching my machine pistol. It is me. I see someone lying on the ground. It is me. Sheets of flame and bitter cold sweep over me.

Albert goes on. Captured by Canadians in Belgium. Escaped. Captured again by Russians. He goes on. But the only thing you listen for now is the bullet that you can't hear.

The Tide

Everyone knows that the tide will go out one day and not come back.
Everyone has stood at the edge of the surf as you and I have.
We listened to whispers become roars become whispers.
The light changed from blue to red to pink to violet to ink.
The cliffs receded into the darkness and the trees disappeared.

And when they are gone we will be gone.
There will be no one left to say,
"They were holding hands."
or "This is where they smiled."

In the morning we washed our hands and faces in the cold creek.
Steam rose all around us. We boiled water for coffee and searched
the sea and sky for the paths of ships and seagulls. There were none.

Somewhere it is raining as much as the flow of Esther's tears
for her daughter dead thirty years ago. What could I do,
Whisper the name on a photograph she carries in her purse?

Somewhere Richie runs in and out of his house wailing to bring his
brother Steve
back from the bottom of the Garden Court Apartments' swimming pool.
Alan, Marty, Barry, Vernon, myself - we all drowned that night.

Somewhere Aunt Eva rises before dawn and wades into Chapman's Lake
with a bar of soap. She will wait years before she succumbs to the
numbing
waters and forget her name - even as I say it to her again and again.

Everyone knows that we are ninety-eight percent water.
So let us hold each other.
And like water poured into water become one.

Fashion Statement

The clothes waited for me
As the fashion statement of my ego grew
    stage-by-stage
To surround me, to adorn me in a prison I would not acknowledge
They waited for my income to bloom
The rich fabrics for my body,
    draped by desire
Waited to give me magic every moment
    to put me to sleep in my waking hours
    to shield me from all I did not want to see
And for my own demise as I became another's reflection
    refusing to see myself
    and the wrinkles underneath
As operators toiled for my appearance
    working, dying
For me the clothes waited on the racks and shelves
    without moving
No markdowns no sales
    they waited,
They waited for me to read the ads
    they waited
As I waited for the illusion
    some way of preserving
    what I never had
    what I could not part with
While every turn of life silently screamed
    clutching at air
While every purchase
    screamed - "The only everlasting cloth
    is your burial shroud!"
Before I understood *Only the naked can be praised,*
Before I realized *The clothes rotted from the my own lies,*
Before I said *I am wearing my prison.*
The clothes waited.

Daymare

She loses all sense of herself in the afternoons. In her glaze, an endless parade of jackets pass before her insisting to be inspected. The speed at which her hands and eyes move over the seams or her nippers trim the loose threads doesn't matter. The clock doesn't move. The jackets come from the left, stay for a while, and leave to the right. At the ends of days, there will be twenty-six coupons neatly pasted on her piecework sheet. She, not knowing how they got there. She sees that the world is made up only of jacket parts: fronts, backs, sleeves, collars… and it is not possible to get to the end of them. The bell rings. She walks to the time clock, waits in line, punches out, puts on her own jacket and walks towards the tomorrow morning of herself.

Woman on a Bed by George Segal

If I look at you from your right side
as you sit on the thin mattress
of an iron cot
you are still, shoulders rounded
lips pursed, gaze focused downward
about to pull on your linen undies

When I move to see you from the back
you are reaching down
hiding your arms, hunched over
so that no one can see what you're doing

From your left side there is
the hint of a smile on your face
and a fond look at your undies

From the front -
From the front -

I can't see you from the front!
the museum has placed
you facing a wall so that no one
can walk around the cot
and see your whole face.

I can't sit beside you,
put my arm around your shoulder,
whisper that I care,
share your suspended moment.

Michael Magee

Main Attraction

They dance in air, on Chinese
fire poles, shimmying to the top,
shimmering, aerialists perform
their escapes in white jump suits.

Clowns with long Italian noses
and Commedia Dell'arte harlequins,
Pantelone, the red-haired woman,
the dancer, the star-spangled pony.

Two strong men, all joint and muscle
balance each other in counterpoint
under the white eggshell circus
tent sky of Cirque de Soleil.

A swinging rope ladder drops down
like a cobra from above our heads
while acrobats launch themselves
like cannonballs into the darkness.

A woman juggles a waterfall
and two bolo dancers circumscribe
the air in arcs to syncopated heels
that go rat-a-tat-tat.

After intermission, a man from
the crowd comes up on stage,
to fight a mute gun battle
to the finish with one of the clowns.

Spider men slide down their threads
in front of us; then fly back up

changing places on their platforms,
execute mid-air passes overhead.
Next to us, they're fastening the lunges,
and a drum beat pounds out the finale.
After the clowns have taken their bows
everyone appears on stage.

We sit clasping each other's hands,
as they rush to their final exits,
we rise wondering what to do next,
with the ground so firmly beneath us.

Cantonese Opera

In Five Acts

It is all gongs and cymbals, the vibrating
bow in our catguts and how, how
our eardrums fill with the pounding song.

Bong. Bong. Bong. Bong.

And the wailing lovers like the cat's meow.
Boo Hoo. Boo Hoo.
We are the mixed-up brothers and sisters who
fall in love with each other,
speak like the treble tongue of the saxophone.
Oh, windy reeds we make with our fingertips
the actors swaying us to hold back tears
in long-sleeved handkerchiefs.

So sad. So sad.

The general has flags up his yin-yang,
the mother who tells her son to kill.
"I want you come back to me!"
Playing upon the polished keys, the striking
of the mallets.

Tick Tock.   Tick Tock.

Birds fly out of the wings, woosh, woosh
to the rustle of a satin kimono
and the clopping of wooden shoes on their
feet like they are fishing boats.
The curtains are calling to you
make sounds with your hands.

Clap. Clap. Clap. Clap.

You're full of luck, rejoice in the happy
circumstance that might allow you to make
a sweeping exit as you circle around each other
tapping elbows, heads are nodding, nodding full of sleep
but the Buddha's eyes are staring
at you.

Blink. Blink. Blink. Blink.

Pointless

The French are all gangsters
at heart, like Jean Paul Belmondo
with a smoking cigar, blowing off
every chance he gets.

Jean Seberg, a striped zebra,
in her turtleneck sweater,
it's useless to protest
not with that smile like an impala.

And his cauliflower ears,
the pug-ugly nose of a fighter
as they romp through Montmarte
at night, not quite sure

Who their enemies are,
stealing cars, killing a cop,
smoking Gauloises, falling asleep
in each other's arms.

He runs down the street,
six slugs in his back,
her dulcet eyes, his derelict hat,
her pouting lips as she watches
his eyes tighten to the close-up.

Life is really a bitch when
you're French and black and white,
before color came along
and ruined the night.

Off the Hook

  for Elizabeth, Paul and Sally

They're tying the fishing line with nylon,
spreading out their tackle in the living room,
with packages of mealworms, and fish eggs,
they have the creel, the dog who fetches your socks
who sits by the fire never moving a muscle,
with their raingear, wellies, ponchos and tents,
they've been ready for hours, risen silent
before first light like King Richard, assembling
and reassembling troops of fishing nets, plotting
out their encampment, No. 167 near Gunthorpe Bridge,
with maps and compasses, a torch for light.
They're tapping and whistling, having a laugh.

Now the dogs are barking, they've packed bags
under their eyes, found the moon down the road
past the soft verges, over the potholes
where they'll wait for barbel and bass, hoping
for the big ones; instead getting carp,
throwing the small fry back, with the nose of Sally
the German Short Hair. If they don't strike
it's the fault of those bloody fish,
who are always going bloody elsewhere for bait,
but they'll tell instead stories of old men
by the river who knew their beds well enough:
the man from Poland who was a spy, he could tell
you where to drop a line, where after the rain
they'd come open-mouthed to the surface, so ready
to be taken, you won't even need to fight.

Bedtime Story

At night he would come to sit on my bed,
my father filling my head with flying dreams
of horses as his voice coaxed me into listening.
I believed everything: the cattle rustlers
who escaped, chased by helicopters,
their blades whirling like gales up the gulch,
and when they rushed from Montana across
the border into Canada, I fled too, spooked
like a Canada Goose, with my head laid back,
on the run, fugitive from my father's arms,
hunted by the mounties on horseback,
free and wild as the cattle thieves;
until he hugged me, hugged me hard,
told me how their campfires alerted the lawmen
and led me to where they hid in the trees.

Sparks flew, wind carried the message back
so that even as they slept, the mounties circled them
while the bandits snored, dreaming of getaways
and cattle cars that filled trains clear to Chicago.
And I thought I was safe too, when he kissed me
and said good-night, leaving me to lie there
my head full of posses, the sleeping outlaw gang
and dreaming of new exploits my father hadn't told me,
the ones he always left hanging
like the noose that always awaited the outlaws.
Now he's gone, where, even he can't tell me,
those ghost riders have crossed the night in songs
so many times, their fires are cold, the trail gone,
he's left only me behind to tell his story.

Greasley Churchyard

"There was only this, the embrace
through stone." — French poem

For Gillie

From here you can see Derbyshire,
follow storms that suddenly appear.
In the Midlands they say: "Wind blows
straight in from the Urals."

The last time, you were wearing
a shapeless sweater, you kept getting
smaller, such tiny bones, your
mother's beautiful butterfly back.

Now as I write you I'm thinking
how headstones give weight, though
I kneel before the ground, tracing
your neck like holy braille.

I remember your father telling me
as he waited at your bedside, holding
your hand. "Dad," you said, "There
are better things than this."

I try to reconnect the letters in
your name, a spell to make you real,
but I can't decipher the codes
that separate us from this world.

Like the lovers in "Women in Love"
who drowned in each other's arms,
we can't let go our lives until
there's nothing left to grasp.

Easter Rising

For Jean

We rise like rabbits from our bed of lettuce,
our cozy warrens and the little nest
you have saved for me with its green
malachite egg, as we stir in each other
still trying to find our legs.

At night, we drift in and out of sleep,
until songbirds come, the breathing
patterns we make before speech;
there is nothing leftover but longing,
Good Friday has been put to bed.

We are full of dew from each other,
perfume from the night before.
We must embrace where we slept quietly,
not even breaking the shell.

Shall I or shall I not ask you,
is it too early or too late, still time
to decide and here I have been waiting
for just this awakening, knowing we have
nothing left to hide.

Carol Shaw

Dream of Home

All the moments come running
To collapse at my feet
Like small children, breathless from playing,
Called in at twilight.
Their eager faces gather around the table,
Lit with candles and spread with a feast.
I beam at them,
Call them to recall, each one, their stories.
Laughter festoons the room and
Swirls of color brighten their eyes
As their hands and voices dance
Through their tales again.
After the bread and butter,
After the meat, the potatoes and greens,
After the milk and wine and
Cake and strawberries and cream,
I tuck them in. One by one,
They drift away to distant lands.
Someday they will dream of home.

The Kettle Sings

Yesterday I slept on the earth.
The sun went into my bones.
Inside the red-lidded cave
I opened my eyes to blue sky.
High over the oasis,
Floating on a wide span of wings,
Flew an eagle.

Today I wrote these words
In red pen on white paper.
Now, at this very now,
You read them.

As though I write these words,
As though you read them,
As though this world is lasting and real.
As though we are all inside the same cave of perception,
Overhead the darkened ceiling
Bursts into blue,
An eagle soaring by again on open wings.

What is real that seems real?
A basket, a woven dress?
Our mouths and hands, fanning the flames of a fire?
The rain falling in rusty fingers
On a red wheelbarrow?

In the newspaper, a photograph of
A woman. She had to flee from home,
Taking only what she could carry.
Cradled against her body, she holds a baby.
On her head, a basket.
Behind her walks a small child
With a bundle of clothes and a kettle.

Imagine you had to leave in an instant,
Taking only what you could carry.
What would you bring?
A basket, a bundle, a kettle?
What vessel holds the inner core of being?
How would you carry yourself?

This I write with a black pen,
Though you wouldn't know
If I hadn't told you.
It is later.
The red pen is lost.
Now I will tell you something else that is true:
Though it might have happened,
Yesterday I saw no eagle.

Time moves in watery waves,
Or distinct molecular memories,
All the atoms rearranged to form
A brief passage of bird wings
Floating soundlessly over a room,
Then receding back into the page.

She walks again, holding her baby,
Her other child trailing after.
Every drop of water must be boiled in the kettle
Before they drink.
If I close my eyes and think of her,
Walking that road,
Dust swirling at her ankles,
Will that alter her fate?

In her path I would place the wheelbarrow
To carry her belongings.
A red fire, to heat the kettle.
And overhead, when she looks up to the sky,
An eagle will lead her to an oasis.

Some see the world in tiny molecules,
Billions of simultaneous motions,
Glittering bits of energy
That know when they're being watched.
What is phenomenal?

I will find my red pen with a rush of recognition
Like the sudden sight of the wheelbarrow.
I will make the kettle sing
Like the cry of an inner truth
So stunning we can almost feel it,
Like the flight of an eagle
We can almost see.

Soon I will stop writing this.
Soon you will stop reading it.
The cave will close over us
Like a blanket of sleep.
Inside we will dream intermittently

Of the woman and her children
Looking into a lens, a chink in the cave ceiling
That lets in a wing of light,
An image in tiny black dots of newsprint.
Ahead of us and behind us,
Compressed along a blue rim,
We will see the long convex road,
The many dusty steps.

Snowstorm

There were all the stories written
And intended
On those winter afternoons
When she sat diligently
Drumming the keys,
The world beyond windows
Rapt in a splendorous wedding veil
Of pinpointed lights swirling and spinning on
Wind and white.

The winter's crystalline cascade
And wild howl lured her
Out into the squall.
She plunged each step
Into a snowy hollow
That marked his footfall:
These were the transitory proof
Of their fine interlude
And strung far, blinding her,
Rushing at her now,
Was a blizzard of stars.

Sheets and feather-down blankets
Swept down, covering
All signs of their passage.
Whirling like words dispersed into night,
As though torn from the fabric of clouds
In pillow fights,
Fell billions and trillions of
Countlessly lovely feathers,
As though she could catch them.

Mermaid's Song

In the original tale, the little mermaid gives up her life in the sea to become human. She also must give up her beautiful voice, she must feel pain as though dancing on knives, and if the prince does not return her love, she must die. The night of the prince's marriage to another woman, the mermaid's sisters cut off their flowing hair in exchange for a last chance to save her. But to return home as a mermaid, she would have to put a dagger into the heart of her beloved prince. Instead, she throws herself back into the sea as mist and foam, believing, before the spirits of the air appear to her, that she will die with no soul.

Where suns can set with no clear horizon,
All streams and rivers rush to reach the shore.
Flung from cliffs, majestic walls of water
Crash into tidal pools that swirl below.
I'm heartened by the waters' steady roar.
For I have danced on knives a thousand times,
I've wound a skein of tales a thousand nights,
I've given up my breath, my voice, my song.
Yet still, inside an unpried lacquered shell,
On a velvet lining rests, untouched, a pearl.

So I shall be jubilant as sea froth,
Dispersed and tossed by churning hurling force:
No boundaries. No sacrifice. No loss.
No feeling but the soft advice of winds
And gentle sway of water swept around
The swirling eddies. Rising into mist,
I'll overflow back to the early yearnings of
The moonstruck blue-green curling crests of a waves.
I'll wait inside translucent orbs of foam,
To laugh as fortune flings me aside.

Sound

In space there is no sound
Except sound that cannot be heard by us.
Here, I hear every word you say.
Pearls dropped one by one
Drift down in a clear green sea.
I breathe in and listen,
My name a gem from your lips.

When thoughts are shaped by your hands,
Word sculptures rise from the paper
Like castles and gardens and the noise of city streets.
The late night scrawl of the rushing pen
Inks long pages over the white-water rocks,
Currents rushing into the stir of
Pages I will fold and unfold again.

A bluebird sings.
I listen, eyes closed,
The feathers of angel wings ruffling my hair.
Then the ceaseless roll of sea begins again.
Summer ends and we walk along the shore.
The leaves rustle their colors
As the trees talk softly of the wind.

The last sound
Is like a pulse beneath the skin.
In the low light our muted voices rise and fall.
I know you by pitch, by tenor — music
Distinctive as the curve of your eyebrows, your smile,
Waiting for the sleep that gathers in the lovely silence of snowfall
With the arms of your voice wrapped around me.

The Queen's Club

"Our lot is such rot," the Queen of Clubs said
In a recent address to the public.
All the King's men chopped her head off again,
Professing to "save the Republic."

The court was bemused, the masses confused,
The King said, "We all must atone.
The knights are alone and the crown jewels quite useless
Without the good Queen on the throne."

Soon, through the work of a seamstress or two,
And deft application of ribbons and glue,
The Queen, reinstated upon her old throne,
Showed no telltale signs of a severed neck bone.

The courtiers arrived, arrayed in their finest.
In deference they bowed down low to her highness.
The good Queen sat stiffly, her face rather grim.
She glared at the King but said nothing to him.

The Line Left Out

Love sonnets spring from many measures we
Have counted. Why count these? Why not delight
In silent spaces wrapped around decrees
Of sound the same way shadows fall from light?
The softened words of lovers in the hush,
Lips whispering on narrow streams of rhyme,
Elude the poet's most artistic touch.
The brilliant gleam of river flows in lines
That wind and meld into the shadowed glades,
As dreams scull into darkness deep as night,
Beyond the flow of syllables we've heard,
Beyond the intertwining of our voices,
Where eloquence abides without a word.

Laura Snyder

Answer

for Murray Gordon

I.

By a window open to sea's breath, rests
a letter on my rosewood desk written
in a strange hand, some *other* language
—old— and signed below, *Murrman.*

Days, I hear the echo, that word, that name,
repeated like a sand-washed shush, an unending thread
like blades of kelp to unseen depths.

II.

A restlessness in spring leaves
drew me to the sea-slashed cliffs
and down the sand path to listen.
I only heard waves and crying birds.

There among cobbles, strings of ulva and torn
eelgrass lay an egg-shaped gem, a swirl
of azure, emerald, sapphire, and grey. Heavily,
it swung from a hand-forged chain.
I stopped it with my hand, then
dropped it.   It was warm.
That night I woke to dark-voiced singing.

III.

Today I am ship-bound, sick, confined
to a narrow bunk and the endless rolling
of a ship bound at anchor. After tears,
I slept. And now, laid before me,
odd-smooth stones, a rose sea star,
colored twists of shell, and sand-scuffed glass.
I know it was you, voice of night, leaver of letters
and sea-cast jewels—driftwood rides on top,
the shape of a man emerging from waves.

Most Nights

for Charles

Without sleep
the window to the deep sky
fills with hours, turning
them over
only calls more.
The hours fall with mussed hair
crowding onto white sheets—
unhappy at being disturbed,
unhappy you won't let them go.

I am here with a candle. The breeze
ruffles the hem of my skirt, tossels the flame.
A gardenia tucked in my dark hair
expands the night. An old man,
with skin the color of a nut, snugs
his guitar close to his belly. His long nails
pull romance out of rosewood and spruce.
Our bodies know this dance.

The F-18 and Convalescence—Day 9

From mom's tall bed

Through the filter of white cyclamen blossoms
before an open window, screams
the pulse-pounding air-greed of an F-18.
I struggle
to an elbow
with pneumonia-bound breath,
and hold   tender eardrums. I was napping.

That Blue Angels fighter
slices the air over Boeing Field,
going so fast—
faster than the sum of all my money,
faster than strep throat which defied every course of antibiotics,
& louder
than complications

to tonsillectomy at forty-four.

Crossing Winter Snow

There was a woman
who walked between two canes,
a risky walk
caught between two worlds.
Her tracks pressed in new snow
made the sign of green grass, but
which is the true solid?

Matter bites with cold teeth,
her body, a map marled blue, confesses.

To cross the snowy road, she stops short
doubting the earth's fixtures. To her
the points of the compass spin
like incense spirals.
She starts again—
one boot down
asking,

then drives   both cane legs
to bolt firm the ground.

Encounter with a Bug before a Basket Class

Between bites of grilled cheese sandwich, I catch
a green shield-shaped insect running the long

spokes of my incomplete cedar basket. This bug
in winter—23 degrees outside—walks on brilliant

spring green legs, fine as hair. Antennae wave
at the top of his head like a conductor with twin batons.

It walks on vertical spokes
up one edge, pauses at the top… conducts a while…

then down the other straight side, crosses
to the next spoke, then on to the next peak in this rectangular range.

I munch away
thinking about those brown fine-jointed antenna,

hydraulics, miniature circuits and the way the natural world
can surprise, invade and bring me into focus—

so many things to wonder at, so much need
to stop   and pay attention.

The bug makes an escape from the cedar spoke range,
so I put out a finger to stop its hurry

along the length of my journal's edge. It takes
to the curved skin of finger, marches

over my hand—so light I would never have known
it was crossing the barren skin of my body—then,

onto my shirt cuff, and across the table,
where it vanishes into the great planet of home.

Juan and the Donkey

There in black and white
steam rises off the coffee.
The bold block print
promises satisfaction—
if you will only drink.

They make the flop-eared donkey stand
beside the written promise—
Juan in the white hat could never convince my choice.
It's in black and white,
and I smell the donkey's sweaty back.

They want me to think in colors,
to hear the happy shouts of peasants
happy to pick all the day long.
To smell the coffee,
they cut trees where song birds winter,
make brown-skinned children work plantations under Colombian skies.

The flop-eared donkey warned me—
his shaggy coat smelled of dust and sun.

Ode to Range Cows—2nd Movement

There you sit
royalty among tall grasses.
The gall of you all
within my gate, within my own fences,
uninvited you recline in splendor.
You turn your great heads,
eyes with no guile
speak   innocence.
Thieves beyond conscience in green pastures
chew cud like some gum chewing adolescent
to cover eighty-five acres of guilt.
You admit to no nationality,
you, the free citizens of the world,
tear down borders that keep you from your seven stomachs.
The ruminations of your trespass
I hear over the truck's running engine.
If I should call out   eviction,
assert my rights of ownership,
you would revenge yourselves upon my fencework
ignoring the wide   open gate.
Yes, I have grass to spare,
but you will not be good neighbors.
You return the favor of my sweet clover
leaving   no   certain   place   for my feet.

Leonard Tews

Northern Lights

I drove away from city lights
out a country road
stood on gravel to watch the sky above.
A firestorm raged on the sun
but on earth it was a summer's night
of owls and metamorphosis of moths.

Laser shots of blue and green, sheer
like curtains in the breath of an open window
undulated, luminously draping and undraping
shadowy like a dancer in dreams.
I yearned for a dropping of the veils
I strove for an intimate peek.

Returning home,
I discovered a cecropia moth
fastened like a brooch
to the kitchen curtain.
With coaxing,
it crept onto my finger.

Cecrops, human thorax, tail of snake
you brought gifts of earth to Attica
gifts of marriage and writing.
Your wings are velvet brown,
you smell of humus, grass fires
and mushroom spawn.

Hubbell, great Earth eye, turns
and turns to catch a glimpse
of the soft primordial light.
We launch another spaceship.
In August we shuttle out
and back again.

Cecrops, still as a marble Hera
you don't reproach.
What is this romance,
our adulterous itch,
this lusting after stars?

Le train à grande vitesse

Alone in Montparnasse station
while waiting for the TGV to Rennes,
a woman sat down at the far end of the bench.
She gave me scarcely a glance.
In age and dress she could have been
my wife except we never spoke.
Then an African boy of ten or so
stumbled down between us and
I thought of my son sitting
between us in the front seat
on our all-night drive to Indiana.
He fell asleep and rested
his head on her shoulder.
She smiled across at me
and I wanted to think she recalled similar trips.
I wondered if passersby thought
he was our grandchild.
Was he exhausted, sick, or on drugs?
I didn't know.
Our little family sat in the station
at peace for half an hour
aboard *Le train à grande vitesse*
where the countryside slides by
at one hundred and eighty miles per hour
and the person sitting next to you
is always a stranger.

January Night, Amarillo

The land is thin here,
the horizon's a pencil line on paper.
Above this line I see a luminous moon
Amarillo stars, and windmills —-
their silhouettes spin at midnight,
their tails turn downstream
like those of catfish.

I know below the line are fossils
of trilobites and tree ferns
pressed in books of bedrock.
In deep caves, there are
blind albino crayfish
with legs akimbo and delicate,
they feel their way along the shale walls.

At the thin surface I hear Coyote,
that old trickster, trotting through
the snowy chollos and prickly pears.
He sniffs the frosty ground for rabbits
then raises his head and yips
at the moon, his breath
sharp in the cold air.

And the windmills turn again
to catch the onyx night
that blows all the way from Albuquerque
to draw up the dark sustaining water.
It trickles into rusty cow tanks
and fills them with moons of quicksilver.
Ambivalent, ambling, I watch my shadow -
again and again, I merge and separate
from the posts and other
shy phenomena in the fencerow.

The Motion that Ends the World

He sits in the food court
baseball cap on the table
forearms blotchy with liver spots
used kleenex in his shirt pocket
support hose dangling from his pant leg.
He has finished his apple turn-over
and dark-roasted drip.

The bump and whine
of Backstreet Boys bounce
from Gap pants, carved African figures
videotapes, and the restless stainless steel
of the escalators of Broadway Market
ascending to the travel agency
on the second floor.
He reads about Freddy Garcia
the twenty-four-year-old
rookie from Venezuela.
There's a picture of Freddy
clear-eyed in a broad stance
throwing his first shut-out
in the major leagues.

With eyes just as brown and passionate
he watches pretty girls pass
in filmy skirts and tattoos
and remembers when he wasn't invisible
when girls watched him in a dry season
in solid Idaho
and sulfur butterflies flew
beneath the bleachers.
He stood
at the plate with his bat held high
waiting for the next fast ball

he loved the order of the game
        the nine innings
        an umpire
        who made the calls.
        Now order is failing
butterflies
        dipsy-doodle across the outfield
        in dizzying dabs of yellow
lighting up sunflowers and goldenrod
        past the travel agency
        out the skylight.
        They fly in a motion that ends the world.

Atheist in Early Spring

Dad is ninety now, and it is mid-winter
but I think of him in early spring
when crusty snow held out
beneath the cedars by the house
and hearing honking
he looked above the barn and saw
that geese were flying –

The strongest bird led the flock
their stern migration like that of Vikings
facing arctic wind and rowing boats
in study rhythm crossing ancient seas.

Dad learned by heart the rigid rules of nature:
he fed stillborn calves to dogs in winter
and drowned puppies with rope and stone.

With boots he shattered puddles glazed at dawn
like window panes to nether worlds
heedless of wind that lashed his face
stiffened his lips and teared his eyes.

He struggled in purple shade
of barn and tool-shed
where steel machines were cold enough
to sting your hand, and frost stood
on the back stonewall.

The strength of men will tell in early spring –
the barn and granary are nearly empty now
and there's a faithless wind around the silo.

He know a wise man's heart is seldom glad –
he shrugs off hopes of heaven or spring's reward:
yellow cowslips bloom in fencerows,
and sweet flags grow amid wild irises.

> *Earth is best, home is best,*
> *hearth is best. And the sun.*

He keeps the world and never minds the rest.

Landscape by Yosa Buson

       Buson filled with emptiness
and seated on a *zabuton*
at low table with blank rice paper rolled out,
begins with the raw feel
of rocks and rivulets,
       and sense of summer mountain.

Brushing rapidly, balanced between
       Dharma and mist,
       his hand, without mind,
raises inky peaks
       to the top of the drawing.
Deft strokes
       of malachite green,
       cling mughus
to sheer cliffs in desperate thirst.
       Pointilistic dabs
tremble aspen,
a few lines wade a woman across
       the icy stream
       suffering with onerous pack.
Further along the path
       is a bamboo bridge,
pale peach fills the bridge houses,
awash with the inner lamp glow
       of early evening.
Two men are crossing the bridge
       the old one stands
and gazes at the stream,
regards a face
       in a house in a window above.

In the upper left,
Buson writes a haiku
wriggling down the page
like squirming tadpoles.
He presses his vermilion chop
        beneath the poem.

Lays down his brush,
rises,
presses his palms together in *ojighi*
bows mindfully and leaves the room.

Bullheads

Brother, what was it?
We were aware.
We felt the breeze
it was as gentle as eider down
stirred the willows and osiers,
carried the smell of marl and mint,
a scent that rose from the mud, pungent and full.

We heard the *basso buffo* of bullfrogs,
the cry of the whip-poor-will.
We saw the sunset running to orange on the lake,
we saw the gold dust on our arms and faces
as we fished with grandpa in the rowboat.

We knew the tackle box with its cunning magic
of hooks, sinkers, bobbers, and fishing line
and learned the sly way grandpa threaded a night crawler
on the hook with his crooked thumbs.

No, it was later on, brother,
when we lit the kerosene lamp
and swung home across the hayfield
with our gunny sack full of bullheads,
that we ignored the shadows
jumping up on all sides like warm ghosts
whispering, *This will pass, this will pass!*

We thought we had out-witted the lake
and thus the world, by stealing her bullheads.
Believed the earth had stopped just
for us, that summer's night.
Dreamed she was an indulgent mother
who'd forgive our theft of grace with kisses
and hold us gently in her arms
like naughty children, forever

Rodney Williams

Adam, Single Creature

And for each animal brought forth
from the god-thing, Adam laid his
trap of words, breath-snare to catch
them up in a single exhalation, fatally—
and all this before breakfast, even before
he had a someone to whom to say:
"The thing… with those things on his…
The what-you-call-it— You know what I mean!"
Until a creature so disturbed his vision
(he thought he saw double, and no time for liquor),
some New Thing turned up after a little nap—
his side aching him and he was ever so breathless—
ran a marathon and hurting him god-awful much—
Now this was a Polaroid moment! Light
having already been made and darkness too
and darkrooms for snuzzling under safelight.
Where would he touch her first? To what
were his eyes drawn, those earthy molecules,
when they fluttered open to see this
new cousin's face blocking the sun?

Blankets

After a night in which I, having executed one-too-many
barrel rolls with blankets, have left the Queen in our bed
covered by half a rectangle less than her geometry would allow,
and the sheets, having been untucked at the bottom
where my longer frame meets
the uncomfortable tightness of her hospital tuck
with a leg kick and a hard rudder to right, and she says this
to me next morning:

You don't know what it's like to be me sleeping with you.

I change my tack the next night, make an effort to take
my half and no more, to scold me in my dreams,
the kind of pre-emptive self-strike a husband makes
to keep a happy wife. And still, the next morning
I hear about it from the other half, how it came untucked
again and how she struggled with tattered sailcloth
to cover a cold shoulder:

You don't know what it's like to be me sleeping with you.

The following night she slumbers first,
a raft of sullen logs in our small sea, a blue sheet
winched round her knees as if to hold taut the sail
and race me round the first buoy of our nightly regatta,
to reach the downwind leg before I swing across her bow,
blanket the wind, leave her luffing and her modesty exposed:

You don't know what it's like to be me sleeping with you.

Next morning, she weighs anchor, goes right down
to the insurance agent. "I want a blanket policy," she says,
"for my husband." The underwriter writes
and all the contingent parts are well covered.

Classified Ad for My Sister

And when my sister
full of her age and needing a good home
placed an advertisement in the Ruralite
and left her fate in the hands of a typist
and a classifier and a newspaperman
with plenty of hands on experience
with the hearts of lonely young rural girls
nearly swallowed by sagebrush and blue sky
and gauzy lace clouds that threatened to come down
and wrap their bodies like shroud
and their faces like veil
and to trail off into a heart-sinking sunset
like a wedding train—
well, this newspaperman, wonderfully drunk
on words and his own ruralization, who once ran away
from a job at the City Desk of a big city newspaper
and left his ambition at that altar,
began to paste the ads from other categories into hers,
and gave my sister a territorial view
and an exciting opportunity with privacy
and great mountain views
wonderfully updated, well maintained, just built—
man, is she built! This cream puff's loaded
with 4 on the floor and hard-to-find
leather, and low, low, low miles—ALL POWER!
until my future brother-in-law
found this lovely charmer of a sister
in the antique section
next to an old watch and drums,
and lots and lots of National Geographics,
most with pages intact.

The Comics

It is that section
that my children fight over
like Kodiak bears
when the Sunday paper
is brought indoors
having landed somewhere
pretty near the front steps
(he's good, this carrier)
and I slit open the clear
plastic sack like a fish
to spill out its insides
on the kitchen table.

A hand, not the smallest,
reaches in
to seize a colored corner,
then retreats to the grassy bank,
to poke a wet nose among the panels
and taste a deliciousness not found
among the hard news and editorials

while I, fish-monger father,
finish the job
by stripping out the advertisements,
the odd-colored and useless guts,
and chuck them neatly
into a bin for recycle—
which I know works because
tomorrow they'll return, unbidden,
tucked among that day's news
like sucker fish
and I hear,
before I'm done with that task,
"Aren't you done with the comics yet?"
from the other bear
who missed the first catch.

Small Traditions in Little Places

There are traditions to be made in the white spaces
and little places, in the stops and gaps of our lives
rounded by shadows and sleep, in the hallways
between Great Rooms and bedrooms where
pictures hang, and my mind, like the stereopticon,
assembles you from 5th grade to 6th.

I see it in the free-hand drawings brought home
in the paper folder from daycare. Abstract monochromes
spun like fixed wheels, every line a circle
and I try to remember what it's like to stay inside the lines
and how little it matters.

I feel it in the end pages of the bedtime book, that brief silence
after "The End" is read and the story settles
like the summer sun at oceanside, its last rays cupped
in small wave-hands leaking water
while the bedside lamp lingers blue in my eyes.

I hear it in the silent notes of a song,
when you inhale and count a breath,
or in the gap of your front teeth redeemed
by a few loose coins tucked beneath a pillow.

And I see it most on Christmas Day when you wake—
a little older, a little younger—to new-fallen snow,
and see the world a cool white blank of possibilities—
before black rubber boots are lifted and set like stamps
and angels are begun by a fall backwards.

I Was Late

I was late
and when my car
a green Oldsmobile 88
followed the six lanes of I-5
bent round First Hill like a large hoop skirt
on the shortest day of the year
at four o'clock in the afternoon
in the rain
I found red brake lights
ranged like Christmas votives
heralding the birth of Christ
—who died a long time ago in just such an accident—
and the rain glistening
made the red lights starry and sharp.

My right leg stiffened on the pedal
and when I slid into the Suburban,
tall and blue equestrian,
I was conscious of the thirst
that had me by the throat
that had me round the throat with red fingers
the thirst that squeezed life's juices from me
like a lemon being squeezed
that crushed my ribs—
I thought then of the chicken pieces
I ate last night for dinner
a thigh and two wings,
as if a thing comes into your head
independent of immediate circumstances,
the need to survive
to climb out of the broken car
before the Jaws of Life
mistook me for rigid metal.

And I loved all people then,
even the saleswoman driving the big blue horse
with a cracked rear windshield,
my chrome bumper now embracing hers
is if they were mating.
While she screamed in the earpiece of her cell phone
and smoothed her wrinkled white dress
the twin towers of St. James
hung over us like stiff Roman soldiers
in crinoline white
and their carillon bells
proclaimed a new hour.

Playing Catch

It's been years since I felt comfortable
in my own skin—I shrunk it once, left it
badly out of shape, like an old woolen sweater
I used to play in loose of an autumn evening at the piano
that wrongly washed looked like it belonged
to a large doll, or a smallish boy with freckles,
and I discovered, once shrunk, this boy came out,
who loved a bit of music himself, though he couldn't play.
And he was to me a father, as the child is
to the man in Wordsworth's poem,
and I gave him some time to talk about his living
while I worried the leather of a baseball glove
to make a deeper pocket,
and we went out to play a little catch
in evening's last gentle light.

His shadow, with the sun to his back
(I let him, so he wouldn't have to squint)
nearly reached mine, though he was yards away,
and the leather made a crisp pop when I caught
his throw. He was stronger than I remembered,
and though he short-armed it like a catcher will
to throw a man out at second, his arm
was accurate, always back to my glove side
so that the labor of each catch and throw
seemed less than the labor to breathe.

Though it got quite dark, neither of us wanted to quit,
so that we almost stayed the game by sound
as much as sight—the 'whhhiiissssk' of ball
slipped through willowy air, the satisfied 'thwack'
of leather, an in-drawn breath, the gathering
of arms, knee, shoulder to oneself,
then a grunt and release into shadows—

Until his mother called our names,
PA announcer reading the lineup card
from the doorway's broadcast, and we went inside
where the light was good and the supper warm.
And I knew then that a boy's dream of baseball
is nothing to a man's,
that there are things he would catch and hold,
tight-fisted, and things he knows he cannot catch
till our life is visited by twilight
and plausible shadows of our selves.

Pieter Zilinsky

Nevsky Prospekt

Van Gogh would have gone,
Gone sane into this city,

> Its alleys, lanes, canals and prospects
> And ordered them into a wooden guillotine;

A frame for all these iridescent Russian dreams.

He would have heard and
> Herded all the flattering, fluttering
> > Tongues and pigeons volleyed back
> > > And forth across the Neva from the spires;

The sky reined in with silver rustling chains.

He would have melted and
> Rounded every drop of pain and fury
> > Nailed beneath a wooden coffin with no depth;
> > > The bloody cobblestones of Alexander's Square;

A wild and flaming free-red cypress.

He would have summoned and
Arrested sprays of salt-streaked cranes,

> Prayers floating up among the god-thrust domes;
> Bulbous fists blown fat with want and incense,

Barred them, hopeful birds, above the sea.

Van Gogh could have come,
> Come mad away from his tame hands,
> > Hands burnt below the sun's sere eye
> > > And plowed his heart into this golden rust,

His mind into these iridescent Russian fields.

Fairgrounds at Washougal

In September when smoke signals the bright demise
Of stubble, husk and stalk deserted in leveled fields,
Crows of the high desert know the picking party's over.
Horses swish and tremble pleasured by relief from flies
And gray dumplings in the sky puff out *Fairtime Fairtime*.

Slim Model Ts greet squat RVs with *Washougal Washougal*
On their horns as solid rubber smears the sidewalks
and traffic mushrooms toward the full flagged fairgrounds.
Walls of dust and denim capped in motley undulate
As "Welcome" arches gulp their sweaty human morsels.

Two blimps, gaseous traffic, undulating side by side, skywalk
Among the smoky dumplings of husk and stalk and stumble
Above the unwalled fairgrounds at Washougal in September.
Cries of *oo – ah, oo - ah* fall from the devil's wheel
On stunned adults admiring a mushroom twirling in the clouds.

Autumn Friezes

When trees decide to drop their leaves
Or see who made the choice to do so,
Whip and silhouette, not crown or bow, appear.

> Stars replace gold peeled from the crown.
> Tripod seeds flutter free against a bare midriff.
> Glancing nuts adorn gnarled feet curled in sod.

When rain attempts to bathe dust away
And fill the web between midrib and veins with silver,
Ricochet and ping displace the whir and splash of leaf.

> Topaz balances on bony willow fingers.
> Onyx coats half a grey torso.
> Agate rolls uncertainly on motley blankets.

When the guest wind whistles a call
To lift a skirt or twist a shawl,
Not a rustle or whisper reply but a lash and whisk.

> Moonstones seal the lance holes in a red helmet.
> White icicles aim at mold sealed on ratgrey bark.
> Blanched flesh shows the loss of a limb wrenched down.

Only a broken fog confesses the secrets of fall,
Easing the limp line and drying edge
Of a variety of apologies no longer green.

> The Milky Way needlepoints a tattoo on a black arm.
> The Pleiades capture a lure cast into heaven.
> Both Dippers hold the promise of springs unpoured.

Snowman

Today my neighbor's snowman had a birthday.
Erect and round a week, he found no one
To pat his head or stroke his nose or belly,
As many freezing fingers did last Monday.
A snowman looks alive but gathers no news.

He attended chickadees' and towhees' sports.
Canadian geese and crows, he saw, flew alien.
His skin, tattooed with squirrels' needled claws,
Was yellow with a message from a pooch
Who paused to etch an echo of his master's voice.

The moon, in jest, showed half its pock-marked face
To mock the black-toothed grin of one who
In a day's golden dalliance turns to tears;
Sweet water from eyes that burn but have
No color. His ears cannot hold a keening.

My neighbor's snowman may stand another week;
Be even moustached and bearded like a walking man
Who wears a crystal memo on a swinging wrist.
Yet, in that fortnight not one snowman in the world
Will recognize sounds of birth, the space of death.

Water

                on the face
                                of it
holds no note
                    of promise,

neither to beggar weeds,

bending over
                                for reflection,

nor to airy-legged walkers
                                that skip too swift

to see
                    their narrow-bellied bodies

shadowed
                                    skywards.

On the face
                    of it

the heady gods

Vishnu, Jahweh, Nereus, Poseidon

enlisted

dancers, singers, smiters and musicians,

Krishna, Moses, Orpheus and Sadko

to tweak
                    their stolid   images,

release
            vital unguents,
                        body fluids

spreading

        good intentions

on the surface

        of their powers.

No rock face gushes,

        no flint sprays showers,

no bloated serpent belly

flushes

        relief

on my parched wish

        to write my name

as Keats,

        fluting so silverly,

did,

        on water;

pleasing Apollo,

        appeasing Lamia.

My last rivulet

        of words,

            imageless,

will drop

        as sumi does

            on silent silk,

leaving

        a stain,

            my echo.

French Horn Flirtation

—for Dennis Brain and Barry Tuckwell

The mockingbird sat.

Above my open-windowed car to —"Welcome
to our festival of horns by Haydn, Strauss, Telemann
and Mozart." — he winked once. I moved the car
two feet closer to decorate the air for him
as he had graced the tree for me.

The mockingbird sat,

immured by the E-flat echoes of a Haydn summer day.
Four horns; east, west, north, south,
each noted a resting boar, unchased, unsnorting,
until the hornists' sharp-tongued attack
announced the call to gallop, yap and pounce.

The mockingbird sat,

not bespattered by the brash splatter of Strauss's
F's or the spray past Punto's lost front teeth.
Held fast in Hampel's fist, firm in the bowels
of the brass bell, the eldrich scritch, *vieux jeu*
and *totus porcus* were denied a hot and cold blow.

The mockingbird sat.

Invited by two horns to feast with Telemann,
a host kind enough to quietly help a lame dog
over a stile, pinkcoats toasted the trophy of the chase.
"Today our entrée is a *tromba selvatica* - E-flat."
Gros ton at such *bon ton* quavered over the table.

The mockingbird sat.

Challenged to scan the riddles of Mozart's wit,
his starling, coached in acrobatic dancing,
put his perch-prints on a staff scored in D.
Blown up by flexible embouchure, heavy birds,
like angels, mount the sky, but do not know how to descend.

The mockingbird sat.

I switched on silence and he twitched
two tail feathers twice; a "Thank You."
Admitting heard horns are sweet
but those unheard are sweeter,
he dropped one mute note earthward.

Lo – Lo

The rain,
shy at first,
began to spell,
drop below
drop,
a long legged
letter,
until tapping the pane
it surprised itself,
rib meeting elbow,
and swept
into a right angle.

A hush interrupted
this mute calligraphy,
as the wind,
refreshed,
no longer paused,
but pushed
its round wet mouth,
the "come on"
of see-through embroidery,
against the leaning L.

In the distance
a broken baton of lightning
punctured a thunderhead.
One prick is all a balloon needs.
The flash, clatter and now
drum drops
spatter onto
a sheet of mock glass,
obliterating any stains
the lovelorn
or lonely
dote on.

Acknowledgements

Grateful acknowledgment is made to the editors of publications in which some of the poems in this book, or earlier versions of them, have appeared.

Pat Duggan: "My Daughter is Becoming the Moon" and "Maternal Instinct" both appeared in *Poetry Ireland Review*, Autumn 2000; "Maternal Instinct" also appeared in *Poets*West; "Summons" appeared in *Seam* (UK), July 2000.

J.Glenn Evans: "Eighteen-Ninety" appeared in *PoetsWest Literary Journal* and in *4th Street*; "Lost Shadows," "Bill and Sherry," "Artful City," "Morford Mann," "The Apple Tree," and "My Father's Hands" all appeared in *PoetsWest Literary Journal*.

Murray Gordon: "Get to Know Your Jacket" appeared in *Raven Chronicles*; "Listen" and *"Woman on a Bed* by George Segal" appeared in *PoetsWest Literary Journal*.

Michael Magee: "Easter Rising" appeared in *PoetsWest Literary Journal*.

Laura Snyder: "Answer" appeared in *The Green Tricycle, #*2, Summer 1999; "Crossing Winter Snow" appeared in *Switched-on Gutenberg*, Vol. 4, No.1, 1999; "Ode to Range Cows-2nd Movement" appeared in *Switched-on Gutenberg*, Vol. 4, No.2, Fall/Winter 2000 and won second place in Charlie Proctor Award for Humor, Washington Poets Association, 1998.

Leonard L.Tews: "Atheist in Early Spring" and "Landscape by Yosa Buson" appeared in *PoetsWest Literary Journal*; "Landscape by Yosa Buson" also appeared in Seattle Art Museum's *Program Guide and Member News*.

Rodney Williams: "Blankets," "The Comics," "Small Traditions in Little Places," and "I Was Late" all appeared in *PoetsWest Literary Journal*.

Pieter Zilinsky: "Autumn Friezes" appeared in *Chiyo's Corne*r; "Nevsky Prospekt," "Lo–lo," "Fairgrounds at Washougal," "Snowman," and "French Horn Flirtation" all appeared in *PoetsWest Literary Journal*.

Contributors

Nancy Dahlberg

Has had her poems published in *Shenandoah, Fireweed, Northwest Review, CALYX, String*Town, and *PoetsWest Literary Journal*. She was selected to read at the June 1999 performance of *Poets*West at the Frye Art Museum. *"My poems come out of personal experience, usually relationships, that has an emotional "hook" and moves me to write about what is happening—the daily occurrence. I find writing takes me on a path of self-discovery which frequently reveals loss of innocence."*

Pat Duggan

Holds an MA in Creative writing from Lancaster University through its branch campus in County Donegal, Ireland where she spent the 1999-2000 school year with her two children. A longtime journalist, she now works as Healthlink producer for KING-TV. Her poems have appeared in *Poetry Ireland Review, Seam* (UK) and *PoetsWest Literary Journal*.

J.Glenn Evans

A former stockbroker, he is poetry editor of *PoetsWest*. Published *Window In The Sky* (poems), *Seattle Poems*, seven community histories, and a *Klondike* anthology. Published in *4th Street, Seattle Writers Anthology, Poet's Ink, PoetsWest, Chrysanthemum,* and *Raven Chronicles*. Received the Faith Beamer Cooke Award, curated Seattle City Council's "WordsWorth." Included in *Who'sWho in America*; is member of Seattle Free Lances, NW Historians Guild, Poets Table, Washington Poets Association (board member), Academy of American Poets, and PEN.

Murray Gordon

Born in Scranton, PA. Anthracite Coal. Smoldering slag heaps. To Philly. Saw swastikas flying from rowhouses pre-Pearl Harbor. To the Beat generation. Poetry. Jazz. To crossing the country. To Seattle. To write. Right here. Right now. Published in *PoetsWest, Point No Point, Raven Chronicles,* and *Sakya News*.

Michael Magee

Is a poet and playwright. His chapbooks include *A Trip to Jerusalem, Ireland's Eye,* and *Duo*. His play *Shank's Mare* has recently been made into a movie and *A Night With Oscar Wilde in Reading Gaol* was produced in England. He toured with Billy Smart's Circus in London. He has appeared in the Distinguished Writer Series and has been a featured reader at the Frye Art Museum. His poems have been published in *POETRY* (Chicago), *Epoch, PoetsWest, Real Change,* and *Poetry Northwest*.

Carol Anderson Shaw

Carol Anderson Shaw lives in Seattle with her husband and four children. Originally from the East Coast, she studied American, English, and French poetry while at Dartmouth College. She worked as an analyst on Wall Street before moving to the Northwest and she still telecommutes to New York as a free lance writer and editor. This is her first published poetry.

Laura Snyder

Laura Snyder listens to old cedars and red-winged blackbirds, mixes cattail pollen with bog mud, coaxes Raven for quills, then tosses her words to the four winds. Her most recent publications appear in *Raven Chronicles*, *Grrrrr: A Collection of Poems About Bears*, *Switched-on Gutenberg*, *Earth's Daughters* and will soon appear in *Tree Stories: A Collection of Extraordinary Encounters*.

Leonard L.Tews

Was born on a dairy farm in Wisconsin and went to a one-room schoolhouse for his first eight grades. A retired professor of biology, he began writing poetry as a legacy to his descendants. After publishing *Family Poems*, he began work on a collection of poems about personalities in his Seattle neighborhood, Capitol Hill. Published in *Fox Cry*, *PoetsWest*, *Point Counter Point*, Seattle Art Museum's *Program Guide and Member News*, *Bellowing Ark*, and *The Wisconsin Academy*. Buddhism, nature and genealogy are important influences in his writing.

Rodney Williams

Was raised in the Horse Heaven Hills of Eastern Washington near where his great-great grandparents homesteaded. He is a graduate of Seattle Pacific University and the Poetry Writing Certificate Program at the University of Washington where he met his fellow poets who formed the core of the Poets Table writing group. His poems have appeared in *Second Essence*, *Wellspring* and *PoetsWest*, where he was a featured reader in December 2000. Rodney works at Recreational Equipment, Inc. in the Information Services department.

Pieter Zilinsky

A native of New York City he was a teacher for three decades. In Seattle he helped develop museum youth programs and worked as interpreter, translator and editor. The diversity of the human and natural landscapes of the Northwest provides a stimulus to move from the mundane to the mystical through poetry, especially spoken poetry. He is affiliated with *PoetsWest*, Poets Table, and serves on the board of the Washington Poets Association. His wife is the novelist, Ursula Zilinsky.

Book design and composition by Mike Jaynes of Seattle.
Computer publishing program: QuarkXpress 4.1.
Display type: Britannic family, designed by Stephenson Blake for the Sheffield Type Foundry in Great Britain.
Body type: Zapf Humanist family (Optima), designed by the German typographer Hermann Zapf.